OIL PAINTING MASTERY

A Beginner's Guide to Brushstroke
Brilliance

Melissa Jose

Table of Contents

CHAPTER ONE

INTRODUCTION

OIL PAINTING FOR BEGINNERS

In this oil painting for beginners guide, we list the essentials, such as the appropriate paints, brushes, and materials, as well as a few reliable extras, to assist you in beginning your exciting journey as an oil painter. To get a handle on what you genuinely need to get all that rolling, this is for you.

Oil Painting for Kids: Second Oil Paint Contains Two Big Plans: Oil Selection and Oil Drying. Oil paint is ordinarily encased in a metal chamber. The most unmistakable size is 37 ml or 40 ml, but a few brands in this way make tubes that are 60 ml, and more essential loads reliably have a volume of around 200 ml. Sums more noteworthy than 200 milliliters are ordinarily bundled in cartridges, which require the utilization of a weapon holder for cartridges to disengage the paint. For teens, a lot of oil paints is an extraordinary hypothesis as it's an impetus and clear procedure for getting an affirmation of assortments across the compass to investigate. A limit of four or five tones can really give you a lot of options if you work on mixing particular sums that are different from one another, as you can see in our Gathering Mixing Series. This could deliver ordinary outcomes rather than working with other assortment tubes, which can really create obfuscated plan mixes. Cases of 'top-end' oil painting sets (**NB:** Several brands infer their most raised levels as "Skilled," while others propose them as "Gifted prepared proficient" grades.) Sets of oil paint are available in Master, Organized skilled and Student grades. It should be seen that the portrayal of these grades isn't obviously clearly self-evident - it is a system for depicting the chance of the paint you can expect from each brand, in spite of two or three appears at fall between what may be considered Master and Organized skilled, or Expert and Student. The detachment between these is that more amazing paints have an even clearer get-together of shade. The gathering is more conspicuous the more certain the shade group. Likewise, other social occasion credits, for instance, surface, body and straightforwardness will decry the individual concerning the reliable paint. For example two or three shades are more retentive than others and will truly need to ingest truly drying oil. The paint that risings up out of this will obviously be more fluid and clear. Paint may end up looking more like glue if a color is less retentive because there will be less end for holding oil. In a nutshell, this suggests that the characteristics of each tone may vary more widely in gifted grades of paint than in understudy grades. Gifted grades typically have a more uniform consistency and grouping energy, starting with one tone and moving on to the next, and the majority of driers stir it up dries at roughly the same speed. This is a variable to consider while picking which brand to buy. I would continually propose buying all that could possibly be worked with for a really exciting diamond understanding, yet if you can't bear the expense of the very best cheer up, as student and gifted expert grade paints are as such prepared for exceptional relationship in the right hands! You can continuously add essentially beyond ludicrous groupings to your set since all grades of oil paint can be consolidated.

FOUR-PIECE JACKSON'S MASTER OIL SET

There a few sorts of oil paint that comes in tubes that are more unpretentious than 40 milliliters, similar to 18 milliliters or 21 milliliters. These are a hair-bringing decision up if you really need a more undeniable level of assortments yet have a consuming mean to stick to. It all comes down to how thick you like the paint to be applied and how many options you have! Regardless, for a one-layer painting (by and large called "alla prima"), you can utilize a colossal number of 12 x 21 ml holders of paint to paint roughly 4 to 6, 30 x 40 cm materials without changing the paint. This would be not exactly satisfactory painting experience to start to sort out your social event inclinations. These paints completely outperform student grade paints in terms of grouping submersion.

Top: Base L-R: Master class St. Petersburg set of eight 18-ml chambers, Gamblin 1980 From the start strategy of nine, M. Graham Dissolvable free game-plan of five tones and two mediums, Master class St. Petersburg set of twelve 18-ml chambers, and Winsor and Newton gifted master oil combination set of ten 21-ml tubes R&F Strategy Stick, Sommelier Oil Stick

Oil sticks are tube shown sticks of pure oil paint encased in wax. They encourage you to use oil paint to draw. Wax pastel engravings are indisputable from oil stick blemishes in light of the fact that, not the least bit like standard oil paint, when applied to a material or board, oil stick marks dry absolutely unaltered. Oil stick engravings can be scattered or gotten along with standard oil paint from a chamber utilizing turpentine or linseed oil.

WATER-MIXABLE OIL PAINT

L - R: Water-mixable oil paints incorporate Jackson's Water Oils, Daniel Smith Water soluble Oil Paint, Cobra Water Mixable Oil Paint, and Holbein Get-together Water Mixable Oil Paint. Water-mixable oil paints permit you to wash your brushes and blend your paint in with both water and oil. Be that as it may, commonplace non-drying oils like linseed or safflower oil will disrupt the paint's capacity to disintegrate in water. The paint will likewise remain water-miscible when blended in with excellent water-mixable mediums and linseed oil. Besides, these paints act in a way that is fundamentally tantamount to that of standard oil paint, making it particularly basic to keep away from the utilization of solvents.

Alkyd Oil Paint, left to right: Gamblin Fast matte Alkyd Oil Paint, Winsor and Newton Griffin Alkyd Oil Paint Alkyd paints are an assortment of oil conditions that dry rapidly and are figured out with oil and alkyd sap, which speeds up the drying system. Near their speedier drying rate they act in basically a fundamentally undefined way to typical oil paint and are other than totally intermixable with standard oil tones.

RISK AND HOW TO SAFEGUARD OIL PAINTING FROM SOLVENTS

One normal misconception is that oil paints are inconceivably hazardous. The majority of oil paints are thought to be safe and have very little strength to make. Cobalt, cadmium, and lead paints are events of fundamental metal assortments that ought to be regulated watchfulness and gloves while what's going on grants. Solvents like white spirit or turpentine, which are typically used to thin oil paints or flush brushes, are the source of the solid exhaust that is typically associated with oil painting. Solvents, clearly, aren't needed for the oil painting process and can be avoided. In the event that you want to clean your brushes without using dissolvable, you can wipe out a lot of paint from your brush by spreading however much paint as could be expected with a surface and a while later flushing as is standard with a brush cleaning capable.

Paint can correspondingly be decreased with free to a more watery consistency. It is fundamental to appreciate that particularly watery thought processes behind weakened oil paint will probably need adequate confining properties. This proposes that the organization surface may ultimately "wear off" the variety except if a layer of stain safeguards it. The more you utilize the paint, the more it will withdraw the oil content. Plus, constantly ensure moderate layers of paint have more key oil content, with the objective that the outer layers are for each situation more flexible and more depleted drying than the paint in the layers under. The standard master's dissolvable is turpentine, a refining of the tar killed from Pine sap. The humble family turpentine is produced by using waste from forests that has been collected from nearby ground. It contains pollutants that have a revolting odor and make it unsuitable for painting; Its obvious elements are flimsy and likely to destroy a secret surface time. Higher grades of turpentine are made with cleaner traditional tar refining cycles and will have a distinctive scent as a result. However, all turpentine's should be used in a well-ventilated environment because prolonged use may result in cerebral torture. Gifted worker white soul is an oil refining, and is fit to reducing alkyd mediums and paint. For the individuals who are by and large captivated by oil painting, the elating smell of turpentine or white soul can agitate. Nonetheless, you can now work with various solvents that don't smell by any stretch of the imagination and are more averse to give you cerebral pains. Pure sol is one such model, a low smell dissolvable that is fruitful in cleaning brushes and lessening oil paint. Gamsol, Sennelier Green More slender, and Zing It are extra models.

Oil paints can be applied with any brush, typical or fabricated, long dealt with or short. Stiffer hair brushes are proposed for brush indicates that you wish to remain recognizable on the material, while milder hair brushes are more fit to blended sections of paint. The long dealt with brush regularly associated with oil painting will allow you to paint from a more conspicuous distance, working with the ability to see the whole of your creation as it emerges. However, when applying fine subtleties, short-handle brushes are simpler to use. Oil painting brushes are generally round, level or filbert formed. I propose placing assets into a piece of each shape, perhaps an enormous and minimal variation of each, so you can examine what marks you can make and which marks you value working with. Using an assurance of brushes on a lone structure can help with keeping your assortment mixes pure and unmuddied from one another, as well as give an extensive variety of brush marks. In order to determine the size of the brush you are looking at online, you should check the actual dimensions of a brush head in millimeters of hair length or width. Keep in mind that there is no standard estimating framework for brushes. These brush sets for oil painting are an exceptional technique for starting a collection.

Ranges

Different sorts of ranges incorporate the New Wave White Cushion Expendable Paper Range, the Zecchi Hand Created Adjusted Wooden Range, the New Wave Cutting edge Range, and Jackson's Glass Range. It is a non penetrable, smooth surface that gives a district to mixing tones. Setting a white piece of paper under a glass section can help with the deceivability of your genuine nature blends because a white range can help with perceiving how the paint will look on a light-colored surface. Untreated wooden palettes tend to be very absorbent and easy to stain when first used. To restrict this occasion you could finish your wooden reach, or rub linseed oil into it, allowing it to dry totally before you use it, more guidance can be searched for in the article How to truly zero in on a wooden oil painting range. The openness of a reach diminishes with use as it comes into contact with progressively drying oil. Oil paints dry steadily conversely, with acrylics or watercolor, so in a lot of events you can leave assortment mixes on your reach to use the next day, however they will start to dry following a couple of days and when dry can be extraordinarily hard to take out. To avoid this occasion you can cover your paint in an impermeable vessel, or add a drop of oil to the external layer of a pool of assortment to keep it useful for longer. Moreover if the oil from a store of paint immerses customary fibers, it will leave the shade sat on a shallow level with no cover holding it set up, which can, for a really long time, make the assortment piece off, or make a yellow brilliance of oil around separated brush marks. The best way to prevent this from happening is to apply oil paints to surfaces that have been sufficiently sized to protect them. Acrylic or for the most part pre-arranged surfaces a portion of the time feel not such a lot of smooth but instead more retentive than oil arranged surfaces. A few unquestionable arranged material sheets could require another layer of clear preparation added to ensure the surface is fittingly fixed this will be communicated in the thing depiction on the web, yet are perfect on the off chance that you want to make the double dealing of painting on rough material. Oil painting papers are either made using an extraordinary added substance which is blended into the crush during creation to make the paper impenetrable to ruining, (for instance, the paper made by Bends) and in this manner are vague from other expert papers, or they are exceptionally covered after sheet advancement. The surfaces of sheets and boards can be smooth, gently finished, or stuck with prepared cotton or material. They are easy to store and transport and are suitable to outdoors painting. Broadened material can be lighter than board (while looking at sizes around 40 cm square and greater) and contain a material made, generally speaking, from fabric or cotton duck that has been expanded immovably and fairly across a wooden packaging. Expanded material is a responsive surface on which to paint; it is most likely going to bounce fairly as you apply strain to it, which can add to the dynamism of an organization meeting. The surface you decide to paint on is completely dependent upon you; in this way, think about whether the surface's weight, unbending nature, surface, and different qualities are significant. If you are unsure, I would suggest giving each one a try to see how it feels. The surface you paint on has a significant impact on the overall experience of creating art as well as the final product. What you choose to paint could coordinate the kind of surface you decide to paint on.

CHAPTER TWO

OPTIONAL EXTRA THINGS ON OIL PAINTING FOR AMATEURS

Easels

You can hang your material or supported board from board pins or screws or tape paper to a wall if you are standing. Then again you could work on the floor or prop your material up on a table. On the other hand, if you have the right easel, you might be able to work with a straight back and avoid unnecessary aches and pains during a long painting session. It could likewise make it more straightforward to move your work to better lighting. While picking an easel you want to present yourself a lot of requests.

Will you be painting at a table? If you will be, a table easel is a moderate contraption that will hold your paper upstanding. Most have a cabinet where you can put your brushes and paints. They are quite easy to store.

Will you need to have a reduced easel? (perhaps for painting out of doorways) If you will be, a drawing easel you'll require. Illustrating easels are regularly created utilizing aluminum or wood. An easy to convey illustrating easel will be lightweight with versatile legs allowing it to overlay into a moderate reduced size. In any case, if you are likely to paint in conditions with a supporting breeze, it may tip over. A couple of string and tent stakes can be a remarkable strategy for getting around this.

Do you truly need an easel that will move to even out? (Will you be using a lot of weak paint, which could run, when you paint?) A couple of studio and depicting easels will move totally to an in any event, working position, which can be really important in case you need to ensure your debilitate paint applications don't run.

Do you truly need an easel that will hold very colossal work? The greatest studio easels are H-frame and firmly stable for craftsmanship's up to 235 cm, yet they will consume room and be significant to move around. The level of your composition can be changed effortlessly with wrench handle easels.

Brush Washer Pots

L-R: The Jackson's Studio Fundamentals Water/Air-Proof Brush Washer, the Jackson's Enormous Metal Select Brush Washer, and the Jackson's Metal Brush Washer are all examples of brush washer pots that are designed to let oil paint dregs from flushing brushes sink to a different compartment, allowing you to get the most use out of your dissolvable. Two Jackson's brush washers have a spring holding structure inbuilt, which holds your brushes so they are suspended in the pot, rather than sitting on the lower part of it, which will wind the hairs of your brush and may hurt them. A brush washer is unquestionably not a central, yet it will help with drawing out the future of your brushes, help to keep your assortments perfect and stunning and besides help to get the most use from your dissolvable.

Oil paint can be used isolated, yet straightforwardness can be extended, sheen changed, and paint can be thickened and made more fluid by adding different mediums. The majority of mediums combine dissolvable with oil or alkyd sap for the addition of various fixings like beeswax or stain. Coat mediums will allow you to make small, clear, sparkle layers of paint, while beeswax mediums help to add mass to paint for impasto methodologies. Alkyd mediums will speed drying, so too will a drop of siccative added to your paint - this is a particularly unsafe cobalt based liquid that should be used sparingly and with care. Countless the trimmings found in pre-arranged mixed oil painting mediums are open in isolation, so you can make your own oil painting mediums to suit your method for managing painting perfectly.

Range sharp edges are incredibly significant for oil painting. They can be used as a choice as opposed to brushes, working with thick impasto usages of assortment that can either be absolutely smooth or significantly wrapped up. They are moreover ideally suited for scratching wet paint away from your show-stopper or reach, and mixing colors on your reach. They are much simpler to remove paint from than brushes; all you need to do is wipe it off with a cloth and your blade will be ready for the next variety blend. They are open in an extent of shapes and sizes, two or three in your weapons will basically help with keeping your assortment mixing composed.

Brush Chemicals

You could go through washing liquid, but brush cleaning agent is especially framed with typical oils to immerse and scour brush hairs, so your brushes save their shape and hairs for longer. Your brushes may become hardened with dried paint at the ferrule if you do not treat them with a brush cleanser. Washing your brushes with brush cleaning agent and warm water directly following flushing in dissolvable is a fabulous penchant to fall into, as you'll be regularly immersing the hairs which will defer their future as well as wash away any development dissolvable which would dry hairs out further. Cover Jackson's Brown Movable Cover Once Phthalate Blue gets on your garments incidentally; it very well may be difficult to get it off. A cover can keep your garments safe and provide you with the inner harmony you really want to focus on the work of art cycle's most significant perspectives.

Bountiful assets can help with promising you have a pencil, eraser or assessing tape commonly inside basic reach. Oil painting is an immensely captivating and overwhelming medium that might perhaps convey exciting masterpieces along with energize them. It very well may be threatening to continue in the strides of extraordinary oil painting Experts; however it doesn't need to be. Start with a few basic supplies, like paint, a dissolvable, brushes, and a material, and see what you can do with what you have. As your interaction makes you may be captivated to endeavor new assortments, mediums, or surfaces, all of which will deal with into how you could decipher your own oil painting tendencies.

TIPS FOR LEARNERS ON OIL PAINTINGS

Experts have been painting with oil paints for a long time and oil paints continue to be notable generally speaking as a result of their flexibility, quality, and assortment. While starting with oil painting is really basic, there is something else to it besides acrylics, since you are working with solvents and mediums and the drying time is fundamentally longer. When an artist has been painting for a long time, they have their own preferred brands, brushes, palettes, and mediums. In any case, in the event that you are simply beginning with oil paints, the accompanying common rules might be useful to you. Begin with

Little Compositions Painting little permits you to explore different avenues regarding variety and methods without committing an excessive amount of time or material. You can get some little 8x10 inch materials or material sheets, or even make a pass at painting with oils on paper. (Make a point to first gesso the paper.

Get Composed

Set up space in an especially ventilated locale where you can keep your reaches and supplies out and ready for action and your things of beauty perceptible. This will permit you the potential chance to see and consider your work, whether or not you're not actually painting. Additionally, it will simplify the most common method of painting, encouraging you to paint more frequently even daily if at all possible. If you paint a lot, you'll quickly see improvements in your work. This is the demonstration of making workmanship.

Put money into brushes. If you can afford it, buy paints of the proficient grade rather than the understudy grade. Capable grade has a more significant extent of shade to latch. Buy several additional fantastic brushes three remarkable sizes should be perfect in the first place. As you paint more, you can buy extra ones and play around with the different shapes. You can use produced brushes made for acrylic paints for oil, but there is similarly an extent of typical hair brushes that can be used with oil. Bristle (crowd) brushes are the most normally used.

Prime Your Material Surface

You can paint on many surfaces material, wood, paper anyway whichever you pick, it's fundamental to apply a kind of starter called gesso to crafted by workmanship surface to hold the oil back from immersing the surface, shield the surface from the acids in the paint, and give a surface that the paint will adhere to even more easily. You can in like manner use pre-arranged sheets or material and apply another coat or two of gesso to them in case you like a smoother surface. Ampersand Gessobord is a charming smooth strong surface to manage.

Interminably assortment mixing

Fundamental paint tones are not "pure" yet rather slant in that frame of mind of either yellow or blue, making them warm if toward yellow, or cool if toward blue. The way the essential varieties combine to produce the optional varieties is affected by this.

Use a Confined Thing of beauty Reach

Make an effort not to feel that you want to include all of the assortments in your masterpiece pronto. Begin with a monochromatic canvas, which comprises of a solitary tone as well as its colors and shades (dark added). You can use any assortment you like dependent upon whether you really want a cool or warm piece. You will actually want to feel the paint through this. Add warm and cool adaptations of every essential tone to your range when you're prepared, as well as earth tones like consumed sienna, consumed umber, and yellow ochre.

START WITH AN OIL SKETCH

This is a thin under painting containing an assortment and turpentine (or unscented turpentine substitute like Torpedoed). Since this will dry rapidly, you will not need to stand by lengthy to apply resulting layers of paint and variety. Replicated sienna is useful to fan out values and construction, whether you work on a white material or tone it with an unprejudiced dim first. Know the request for the paint: paint thicker than slim, fatter than lean, and slow-drying over quick drying. That suggests including more thin paint and less oil in the essential layers, saving thicker paint and higher oil content for later layers. This will assist in preventing your artistic creation from breaking and ensuring that the previous layers dry first. Prior to continuing on toward a work of art medium made out of a 2:1 proportion of turpentine to linseed oil, start with an under painting of paint and turpentine. Linseed oil can yellow with age (which is clearer on light tones) but dries faster than various oils.

Clean Your Brush

It's basic to clean your brush among colors and with chemical and water while finished the most common way of painting. Oil painting can get jumbled. Have paper towels and garments supportive to clear excess paint and turpentine off your brushes. Have two holders available while painting one for turpentine for cleaning your brush among assortments and one for medium to mix in with your paint.

Keep It Clean

Oil paints and mediums are hazardous at whatever point ingested or held into the skin. They should be secured and kept out of children's reach and pets' reach. Paints, mediums, clothes, paper towels, and disposable paper ranges or plates which can also be used as ranges should all be disposed of appropriately. You should wet or ingest garments and paper water preceding discarding them since they are ignitable, can heat up while drying out and sometimes quickly combust.

Steps toward learning how to paint in oil Straightforwardness, radiance, material effects, meticulous detail work with oils, your options are endless Six crucial steps to guide you through painting in oil

1. Choosing a topic

• Is it safe to say that you are just getting started? Cultivate your hand on essential subjects, for instance, still life. Later, you can handle more difficult topics like pictures and scenes.

• Use a photograph so you can work without watching the clock and, if you don't have even the remotest clue how to draw, for following your model onto the medium.

2. Structure of the painting.

• Find a main line that interfaces the different scene components lines, shapes, varieties, and light to a brought together entirety. Use your sense; it's your best accomplice.

• Peculiar focuses will add to the interest of the material. Notice your subject, focusing in on a detail or taking in the whole scene. To do in that capacity, use a window cut out of cardboard or construction an edge with your hands. If you are working from a photo, use segments of paper to reexamine it.

• Assess your contemplations on paper: change the outline and the exchange of shadow and light as necessary.

3. Draft

This is even more an "outlining guide" than a total drawing. In spite of the fact that it isn't needed, this step can be exceptionally useful when you are prepared to start painting.

• Sketch your subject on the medium with charcoal (make sure to shower on a fixative) to keep your paint clean; then again delicately with a pencil, so it doesn't show up through the paint; or, alternatively, using oils or acrylics in a very neutral, weak variety.

• Might it be said that you are feeling unsure of your pencil stroke? If you are working from a photo, characterize the critical limits of the model using the structure system or following paper.

• Use clearing lines to record the crucial parts: Assuming that you attempt to steadfastly portray the scene down to the smallest of subtleties, you will pointlessly overburden your work of art.

Mostly secret strategy

Notice the subject with your eyes half shut, so all you see are spots of assortment and dim masses. This helps you with disregarding superfluous nuances and work on the designs making it.

4. Principal layer

For paint to stick well and dry without breaking, you truly need to gently apply an establishment.

• White or toned? A white foundation is great for heavily shaded subjects because it illuminates concealers. a concealed establishment gives a secret tone to unite the structure: pick the assortment in view of the last tone you accept that the material ought to have (hot, crisp, light, faint...).

• Make use of a lot of weak paint and wait for it to dry before moving on to the next stage. You can similarly use acrylic paint, which dries speedier.

Unobtrusive technique

To check whether the establishment is dry, delicately run your index finger in excess of a couple of spots; if it gets no paint whether or not the surface seems, by all accounts, to be tasteless you can add the accompanying layer.

5. Applying layers of paint

Concealing a synthesis is done by superimposing layers. Start by adding areas of shadow and light, fill in tremendous districts with assortment, then, at that point, work tranquilly, laying on an always expanding number of uncommon layers of assortment.

• You truly need with comply to the splendid rule of oil painting: portrayal "thick on slight" Each succeeding layer should be barely "thicker," that is, contain more oil, than the beyond one. The principal layer ought to be much weakened, and the resulting layers ought to be steadily less weakened. Anyway, you risk having your organization piece after some time.

• The second essential rule: believe that the layer of paint will be totally dry preceding applying the accompanying one. Experienced painters can use a different, quicker method: the painting "alla prima." This methodology is used outside or to get the abruptness of a scene; it licenses you to finish your masterpiece in a single gathering, because each layer of assortment is applied over the beyond one while still new.

6. Last layers and finishing up

A painter's real work is completed here. This includes using light strokes rather than slapping paint on. This is assigned "making the material sing"! It's the last fitting of tones.

• Use undiluted paint, straight out of the chamber.

• Stand back routinely from your piece to evaluate it. Be the most memorable viewer of yours.

• Make an effort not to hustle! Change your piece dynamically, add lights, work on the shadows, and refine the nuances. At this stage, any tremendous change in assortment remembers changing all of the shades for the craftsmanship.

CHAPTER THREE

TIPS, MATERIALS AND METHODS OF OIL PAINTING

Exactly when you paint with oils there are two or three guidelines to keep ensuring that your materials persevere through regular difficulty, and various juveniles are put off endeavoring oil paints since they envision that the procedure is excessively muddled to try and contemplate ruling. It tends to be very scary to look for guidance on painting gatherings, where you can find extended conversations and various perspectives in regards to paints, mediums, and preparing arrangements and their application. In this post I will endeavor to set out a couple of really fundamental step by step controls for the complete youngster, as essentially as could be expected. I trust this will give you conviction to buy a lot of oils and get painting! We'll cover which materials to use, what to really focus on while making procurement of oil paints and painting gear, and a couple of fundamental methods for either layering or painting in all cases go (you can jump straightforwardly to procedures here). There are certainly no paid associations here, essentially a couple of free thoughts for important things.

PICKING AND SETTING UP YOUR MATERIAL

I will hope to be here that in the event that you are a fledgling you would prefer not to either extend your own material, or apply the estimating and getting ready to it yourself. If you become genuinely centered around oil painting in future there could clarifications behind do both of these, but while you're starting it's much more straightforward to buy a pre-broadened and pre-arranged material that has been totally set up for you. Monetarily coordinated materials return to the degree that the Impressionists who as often as possible worked on them, so you are emulating some splendid individuals' example!

Sorts of material

You'll need to pick between managing a standard broadened material, a 'material board' or a 'material board'. Sheets and boards are typically designed either for training canvases or for painting outside of entranceways. They are intended to be smaller, lighter, and more portable. Material sheets are open in multipacks and are ideally suited for drawing and examining, yet since they are for the most part truly temperamental and delivered utilizing non-credible materials, they are best avoided expecting that you accept the work ought to make to aft looking good for quite a while. In order to protect the material from the corrosive in the board, boards are made with more enthusiastically sheets of some portrayal and may be made with chronicled paste. In fact, examine the mark to determine whether it is free of corrosive. In the event that you purchase a standard extended material, you should pick between a cloth material or a "cotton duck" material, which comes from the Dutch word "doek," and that implies fabric. Materials made of cloth are inclined toward by numerous experts because of their solid and versatile weave and more tight weave. This suggests that they are worse than cotton or that there's anything not right with a cotton material, and to be certain you could incline toward the coarser surface of cotton. Whenever you've chosen cotton and fabric you'll need to pick between an extra fine, fine, medium or brutal weave. This is really an issue of individual choice. Assuming that you profoundly want to do finely point by point painting a smoother weave will suit you better, while on the off chance that you keep up with that ought to do free and expressive work you could get a remove from the opportunity to see and sincerely stress the material surface. If your material feels a piece slack and not 'springy' enough, use the little 'material keys' that show up in somewhat back stapled to the back of your material to set it up. Jacksons have a fair informative activity on the most effective way to do this.

Assessing and planning

Pre-stretched out materials should constantly come totally assessed. Assessing is the demonstration of covering the material with either a bunny skin stick, an acrylic polymer size or a PVA plan to seal the strands of the material, shielding them from acids in the oil content of the paint holding them back from ruining as the paint continuously dries. Most monetarily expanded materials will in like manner be pre-arranged, giving you a stunning white fruition that is ready to work onto. Planning gives additional protection to the strands and moreover gives a smoother surface, fixes the material, and stimulates extraordinary obligation of the paint layers. You are not really required to work on a prepared material for as long as it is adequately estimated, and some people prefer to work crudely on a plain material foundation that they allow to remain visible. To work onto an unprimed material there are some lengthy fabric materials available which are pre-sized with stick anyway not ready. These are regularly suggested as 'stick estimated' materials. Getting ready is a fairly bewildering district. Most set up materials will communicate that they are 'Triple ready with three layers of gesso' which truly suggests that they have been arranged with an overall acrylic-based foundation sensible for painting with either oil or acrylic paint. This kind of getting ready habitually known as 'Acrylic Gesso' doesn't anyway have a say in certified gesso, which is a standard blend of glue size and gypsum. It is occasionally presented simply as "Widespread" foundational work. Some serious oil painters prefer to purchase "oil prepared" cloth materials, which are available at a cost, because they believe it is safer to work with a material that has been prepared using an oil-based preliminary rather than an acrylic one. In any case various painters are thoroughly happy with a by and large pre-arranged material yet some will give their material an extra layer of primer if they feel the planning layer is too thin and the material sickly in snugness and too absorbent.

Reducing your paint

We ought to now talk about how you truly apply your oil paint. You can clearly apply your paint straight out of the chamber, yet it will be strong and dry. Assuming you really want to paint thickly in an 'impasto' style there are various mediums you can mix in with your paint and we'll cover impasto painting in greater significance further down. If you don't expect to paint with incredibly thick paint them you should debilitate your paint a little to make the right stream. Oil paint is regularly diminished with a feeling of some sort (dissolvable), and different oils can likewise be added to help it stream and expand. You'll need to get to know a dab about how to change the two.

Reducing with spirits

Standard oil paint is totally insoluble in water, which can't be used to debilitate it. A color and an oil fastener, such as linseed or safflower oil, make up the oil paint that comes in your cylinder. To thin your paint to make it stream even more successfully you could simply choose to add a more noteworthy measure of one of these sorts of oil, yet your paint would promptly end up being smooth and glossy which isn't exactly a look (or surface) that you want. In addition, because oil paint gradually dries, it's important not to use too much oil in any under layers because you might break your composition. We will examine this issue more meticulously in a second. In the several layers of paint applied straight over the planning layer, the best method for diminishing your paint is with a dissolvable, for instance, 'Expert's white soul' which is a portion of the time similarly portrayed as 'mineral spirits'. Make an effort not to be captivated to use ordinary white soul that you can buy from a DIY store since this will contain corruptions that could hurt your paint layers. From here onward, indefinitely a truly prolonged stretch of time the standard soul for debilitating oil paint was turpentine and you can regardless buy this yet it's truly destructive and by far most prefer to avoid it. If even experts' white soul gives you cerebral agonies or you are particularly stressed over noxiousness then there are low aroma things like Winsor and Newton's 'Sansador' or Gamblin's 'Gamsol' which are still petroleum-based at this point have had fragrant combinations taken out and scatter significantly more comfortable. There are similarly a couple of new solvents refined from citrus natural items which case to be non-destructive. Numerous people will use spirits to clean their hands, brushes and ranges too, notwithstanding the way that there are gentler approaches to doing this with the usage of things that consolidate vegetable oil-based cleaning agent, for instance, 'The Master's Cleaning agent' or 'The

Master's Brush Cleaner' made by Wide Pencil or Jacksons' 'Marseille Chemical Pellets'. Da Vinci and Escoda also produce skilled workers' oil cleaning agents. The "Turpenoid" brush cleaning items from Weber are produced using a scentless, non-harmful, and exceptionally compelling substitute for turpentine.

Reducing with oils

People could choose to debilitate their oil paint with the development of extra oil to make petite covering layers, to assemble the clean of their paint, or to either speed up its drying time or tone it down to control the paint for longer. Linseed oil is the praiseworthy choice for oil painting yet can be a little yellowing in this way safflower, walnut or poppy oils are a prevalent bet for whites or pale tones. The majority of the time, linseed slows down the drying time of your paint, but modified "Quick Drying" linseed or poppy oil will speed it up. Stand oil' is a thickened linseed that is truly perfect for making even, smooth coatings. A well known thing by Winsor and Newton called 'Liquin' is an alkyd-based plan expected to debilitate oil paint and accelerate and thickness. Liquin isn't an oil (alkyds are oil-changed pitches, fast drying and semi-matt) and besides contains an unassuming amount of dissolvable yet performing more like an oil medium than a dissolvable more slender is arranged. It is preferable to use it on the upper layers of a canvas rather than the under layers, where it should be used sparingly.

THE AMICABILITY AMONG SOLVENTS AND OILS

If you add a great deal of dissolvable to oil paint to thin it, you may just so happen to debilitate the oil content of the paint to where it becomes unbalanced and doesn't adhere well to the material when dried to a film: this is called becoming 'under bound'. When this occurs, there is a possibility that your paint layer will become temperamental as it dries, making it ineffective against chipping and breaking. In this manner when you debilitate paint with spirits you need to all the while add very nearly a similar proportion of oil. This isn't needed in the principal layer of paint because the essential layer will sink into the getting ready layer where there is a ton of oil. Your most memorable layer of paint can thus be weakened by spirits alone. For coming about layers you need to balance any extra solvents with extending proportions of oil. This is the famous 'Fat over lean' conclude that we'll look at this point. If you are decreasing your paint with Liquin, there isn't any need to add extra oil to change the dissolvable substance, in spite of the way that Winsor and Newton propose applying layers containing a ton of Liquin pitifully and as we've recently referred to they suggest using it sparingly in lower layers. It's open in different setups including a 'fine detail' version. W&N in like manner make an 'Experts' Painting Medium' which is a blend of both oil and a dissolvable, and moves back drying time rather than speeding it up. Schminke's 'Medium W' gel is another alkyd based elective which doesn't speed drying time. It can be washed with water and a cleanser.

CHAPTER FOUR

THE "FAT OVER LEAN" RULE

The significance of the word "fat" in this context refers to the amount of oil contained within the paint layer. A layer with virtually no additional oil is considered "slim," whereas an oil-weighty combination is considered "fat." To totally grasp the Fat over lean rule it's important to have a hold of why it's huge. Exactly when you apply your paint mix to your material, the foremost thing that happens is that any dissolvable you have added disseminates. This occurs fairly quickly. Meanwhile the oil cover added to the variety to make the paint notwithstanding any extra oil you've added yourself begins to oxidize, and as it does so it starts to dry and set. While the paint could feel contact dry on a shallow level inside the space of days or weeks, the course of the oxidization of the oil content takes from a genuine perspective quite a while to totally get done (a cycle known as 'easing'). As oil bit by bit oxidizes it contracts, and thusly the paint layers will continue to 'move' for a surprisingly long time before they are totally feeling better, during which period they will be unsteady. Almost certainly, the paint on the upper layer will break on the off chance that a layer of paint dries quicker than the layer beneath it. Thus the targets of the Fat over lean choose is to ensure that each layer dries fairly more relaxed than the one(s) above it. The more oil a layer has the more it will continue to break as it dries and the more versatile it will remain eventually. Your point, then, at that point, is to make slow drying layers over speedy drying, somewhere around ones versatile layers over less versatile ones. Layers will anyway oil from the ones above them, hence set up all in sensible terms the Fat over lean conclude suggests that no layer of paint should have more oil added to it than the one above. Remember, solvents make paint small, and oil makes it fat. Having a tremendous and stable oil content in an upper layer is something that would merit being grateful for because the upper layer will be the most vulnerable against hurt regardless, when totally reestablished hence flexibility and extraordinary grasp in the upper layers from a great deal of oil is a positive thing. In most cases, you won't even need to add any oil to the first layer. Instead, gradually increase the amount of oil in each subsequent layer. If you are using a very oil-profound layer to make a shrewd frosting (glazes are usually used in the depiction of water, lavish surface, glass, jewels, and so on) this should be without a doubt the last layer. Realize that a covering should be humble, for the most part a unimaginably smooth layer will wrinkle. Another huge part that impacts how fast your layers will dry is the way thickly you apply them, in this manner you should in like manner consider similar to 'thick feeble', keeping your lower layers more thin and saving the use of thick paint for upper layers. It's best not to apply a thin layer of paint over a thick layer of impasto because it will eventually fall off. If you are working with a thing like Liquin which at this point contains both an alkyd substance and a dash of dissolvable then you don't need to add extra oil as you apply coming about layers yet it's reasonable to use just a smidgen or no Liquin in your most vital layer and add fairly more to each layer on top.

Could oil-based painting be managed without the utilization of solvents?

For sure on a basic level you can and numerous people do, disregarding the way that you won't have the choice to make humble washes for any under layers likewise you could by mixing in with spirits and a drop of oil. However long you apply significantly more oil to the layers above, it doesn't make any difference how much oil you use in the under layer: this would anyway submit to fat over lean. It would help with leaving your lower layers longer before painting on top to give them an early benefit on drying.

THE MOST EFFECTIVE METHOD TO APPLY YOUR PAINT

Working in layers Paying little heed to how you need to paint in oils, assuming you intend with utilize more than one layer, you should comply to the "Fat over Lean" rule. Aside from that, there aren't really any additional instructions for painting. There are in any case different practices for laying on your paint which may be helpful to find out fairly about. We'll next look at the differentiations between painting wet-on-wet ('direct unendingly painting in layers ('underhanded canvas'), and different decisions to apply a concealed establishment and work with some specific under painting procedures.

WET-ON-WET OR 'ALLA PRIMA' (DIRECT CREATION)

Defied with your white arranged material, you may be totally happy just to contribute and start applying paint, and to apply all of your paint before any of it has dried. This system is notable as 'wet-on-wet', or 'alla prima' which can be deciphered from Italian as 'first undertaking' or 'pronto'. In French, it was called "au premier coup." There is some chaos about the certified meaning of 'alla prima' and whether it on thoroughly depicts a creation completed in one gathering or not (this gives off an impression of being outlandish because oil paint stays wet and valuable for a seriously prolonged stretch of time) and moreover whether or not alla prima includes working in a single layer. Some will battle that it can regardless encompass a show-stopper made with a degree of layering for whatever length of time paint was applied over other paint that wasn't yet dry. However, you have the option of applying your paints wet-on-wet in one of two ways, either wet into wet or wet onto wet, if you need to work extremely quickly and directly with almost no foundation tone and possibly no "drawing out." You'll get a very liquid, fluid effect that could a portion of the time at any point be fairly level with no under painting assortment mumbling through various layers. Despite the fact that it was covered up a few sittings, this flawlessly executed painting by John Vocalist Sargeant utilizes wet on wet composition with practically no under painting. With direct imaginative creation if don't actually keep up with that your assortments ought to blend as you apply them to your material you'll have to do whatever it takes not to make them unreasonably runny and smooth. If working in a single layer you could thin your paint pleasant to you with Liquin, Medium W or W&N's Expert's Painting Medium, or just with barely enough spirits. To prevent your paint from becoming unbound, you should offset any spirits that have been added to your paint with an oil. If you want to cover wet up wet in a very layered manner, you should follow the Fat over lean guideline. If you prefer to paint thickly and obscurely when painting alla prima, check out some of the "Impasto" mediums we'll look at below to broaden your paint and get a good stream.

One more thing to keep in mind is that there is no good reason why you can't use one layer of wet-on-wet paint above a single layer of colored under layers. The final layer of paint in many layered compositions will have some wet-on-wet work. Albeit most of Impressionist works of art seem to have been finished alla prima with wet paint, they really contain either blocky under painting or layers of paint under. Expecting you have the astonishing opportunity to look at organizations by Claude Monet close up you'll see that he uses unreservedly stumbled paint over more controlled and dried paint layers under. Detail from Heaps, end of summer by Claude Monet, 1891. Compositions (circuitous work of art) The most common way to apply paint is to work in layers and wait for one layer to be contact dry before applying more paint on top of it. This is called "circuitous" painting. Experts would begin with a concealed under layer before, when in doubt, using some sort of under painting technique including closing out areas of wide paint, lastly refining their show-stopper and their better nuances on top. Much of the time a part of their layers would incorporate a degree of straightforwardness with murky, clear, or scum bled paint revealing dried paint under.

CONCEALED ESTABLISHMENTS/MOLDI NG LAYERS

There are different inspirations driving why you ought to add a shaded establishment layer to your material. Apparent connections and varieties can be challenging to decide before a splendid white material, particularly while painting metaphorically from perception. Consequently, many artists prefer to begin with a color layer whose tone matches the mid-tone values of the painting. Adding a colored foundation may also have additional advantages. At the point when applied over the entire masterpiece, a principal 'molding' assortment can present a sparkle and clear fortitude to the layers above it by reflecting or uncovering it through coming about layers of shady paint or scum bled paint. Generally skilled workers habitually covered their getting ready layer with a layer of debilitated paint called an 'Imprimatur'. This would stain the pale concealed getting ready ground to make a mid-molded establishment which would unite the assortments applied above it, making an overall clear air and a significance and dynamic quality. Imprimaturs were a significant part of the time applied in an 'earth' assortment to give a warm tone anyway you could moreover apply an establishment layer in a fair-minded dim or a cooler shade with some blue in it. This work by Whistler shows the usage of a warm brown Imprimatur, revealed in the fragmented lower half of the material. Hunterian Craftsmanship Display, Historic Center of Glasgow Another option is to block in large areas of various level tones to distinguish the various components of your composition rather than using a single variety across the entire canvas. This was a procedure often used by the Impressionists and was close to the 'Ébauche' system for under painting that we'll look at in a second. The main layer of paint you apply on top of the white groundwork will dry more leisurely than ensuing layers since they will sink into the layers beneath them. In the event that you don't matter the paint meagerly and work it into the material with your brush, you'll need to stand by above and beyond seven days for it to be contact dry. This paint layer needn't bother with any more oil since it will be consumed by the preparing underneath it, which as of now has a ton of oil, and in light of the fact that you ought to observe the Fat over Lean guideline and not put a lot of oil in your most memorable layer of paint.

Under painting

If you are doing a really standard non-strict structure, how might you draw your arrangement onto your material? You could hypothetically achieve this with pencil or charcoal, however you risk blending graphite or charcoal in with the paint you apply on top and turning it dark in the event that you have previously settled a shaded under layer. It's conceivable that you simply need to get everything rolling composition without drawing. However, a lot of people like to do some kind of under painting, whether it's a simple sketch in lighter paint that helps them "map in" different areas of their plan or a more substantial shut out under painting that helps them distinguish between light and dark tones and may even deepen their previous paint layers.

There are different techniques of 'under painting' that arose out of different imaginative creation customs. It's significant to be have some familiarity with several the most prestigious strategies since you'll every now and again run over references to them relating to oil painting, disregarding the way that there's convincing explanation need to follow them in case you would prefer not to.

1. The expression "grisaille" under painting alludes to the utilization of weakened paint in a dim or gritty tint to hinder in light and dull regions. For the most part 'grisaille' implied a dim concealed under painting and 'burnable' to a hearty one, but today the term is used on the other hand for any monochromatic under painting. If a faint containing a white shade was used this was habitually suggested as a 'dead assortment' layer. A grisaille layer can look

exceptionally free and questionable or like a total desaturated painting or high contrast photo. On top of this conveniently unfinished portrait, Gainsborough used very thin paint to apply a warm Imprimatur layer with some sketchy grisaille-style under painting.

2. 'Ébauche' under painting, from a French word meaning 'first pass' is a sort of concealed under painting where areas of possibly desaturated, fairly dull washes of petite tones are used to spread out colossal areas of different designs in something close to their certifiable assortment. Sometimes, it is alluded to as a "lay in" of paint. This work demonstrates the utilization of ébauche-like under

painting as part of a composition by Benjamin West that is largely incomplete. A more current way to deal with working is to simply paint in totally drenched, really dinky blocks of assortment for your lower layers. You can then either totally cover these blocks, or license some of them to shape your faint, light or mid tones. I paint my under layers unmistakably depending upon what I'm painting: For complexions, I normally start with a lighter under layer and develop my varieties, while for dress; I pick an exact mid-tone and afterward apply shadows and features. Anything methodology works for you is absolutely fine. Painting Impasto basically alludes to the most common way of working with incredibly thick, inflexible paint. It's a procedure that you can use in both wet-on-wet or layered painting, giving you holds it to your top layer. Impasto painting ought to be conceivable with a reach edge instead of a brush. It's consistently felt that Rembrandt was potentially the earliest specialist to apply his delightful textural paint with an edge, and Van Gogh is more present day model. On a basic level you could make Impasto basically by using paint smooth out of the chamber. There are a couple of issues with including your paint thusly, nevertheless. Not exclusively will it be extravagant, however your paint will likewise consume a large chunk of the day to dry on the grounds that the paint outwardly of a thick mass will dry quicker than the paint within. This could bring about a surface that is creased. To get a superior Impasto impact, you can change it up of mediums to your paint. Beeswax glues are famous, and Winsor and Newton makes two sorts of fluid medium that dry rapidly and can be utilized to thickly paint: Oleopasto, which has a semi-matt completion in the wake of drying, and their Impasto gel, which is a fluid, has a glossier completion. W&N propose using an extent of one segment Oleopasto or Liquin Impasto to two segments oil paint.

CHAPTER FIVE

GUIDELINES TO APPLY YOUR OIL PAINT

Oil paint can be applied in different ways and not just with brushes! Could we look at the different decisions Oil painting brushes? The ordinary brush for oil paints is delivered utilizing pig hair which is strong and springy and hailed (split) close to the completion of every fiber. It is therefore strong enough to manipulate oil paint while also being able to carry a "reservoir" of paint and smoothly spread it. Crowd hair brushes are quite easy to perceive from their real pale or white blurred assortment and will often be made with extra extended handles so you can avoid your easel as you paint. Although it is difficult to replicate hoard bristle with an engineered brush, there are a few good-quality ranges available made with polyester fibers that mimic the firmness, shape, and tiny surface of hoard hairs. However, I am unable to locate any that are particularly significant areas of strength for a hair as springy as regular hoard. For better subtleties or coating, a few craftsmen like to utilize a gentler brush. I suggest either a synthetic brush made for acrylic artists or a black hog bristle brush that is softer than regular hog for this purpose. Made Mongoose brushes are also perfect for better nuances in oils.

Range cutting edges

A reach cutting edge or two are a certain need for oil painting. They show up in different sizes and shapes: some are truly rectangular with twisted corners and others are exceptionally pointed. Range cutting edges are unfathomably versatile. They are created utilizing a fragile and bendy metal so other than the way that you scratch off can any mistakes from your material with them yet you can moreover apply your paint with them if you are working in a thick impasto style (Rembrandt presumably applied a lot of his paint with a reach sharp edge). They are in like manner an especially supportive studio instrument for scratching paint around on your reach and scratching it off when you've wrapped up with it. Mixing your tones in with a reach cutting edge is very useful and saves your brushes from separating quickly.

Silicone painting devices

Silicone 'painting devices' or 'assortment shapers' comes in different sizes and shapes. You can scratch into thick paint and make intriguing surfaces with a considerable lot of them because of their minuscule edges.

Mixing your paint

Everyone has a profound knowledge of a standard wooden expert's reach and fair oiled walnut ranges are truly unobtrusive to buy. When you buy another wooden range, you will need to "condition" it by rubbing some linseed oil into it several times with a cloth to seal the wood and make it less receptive to moisture. To save yourself a lot of cleaning you can moreover buy nonessential oiled paper ranges. These capability honorably and are especially useful for painting out of entrances when it would challenge to clean up a wooden reach to send it back home. Some people prefer to use ranges made of glass or clear acrylic, which are easy to clean and let you see the color you're blending even if you hold the range over your material to see the color you've applied in advance underneath. Putting my varieties on my range in order of their variety groups (reds together, then, at that point, oranges, yellows, greens, etc.) rather than arranging them haphazardly is a helpful tip from jacksonsart.com. It saves such a great deal of time looking at the reach when I want to track down a particular tone. Whether or not you expect to use a minuscule number of assortments, coordinating them in a comparative solicitation on the reach each time will make it more clear to find the right tone quickly. I save some space in the reach for making blends, and put my whites in the middle since I use them regularly to variety various assortments.

Be careful so as not to waste paint by putting out a greater mass than you truly care about. This is so normal to do and you really need to set yourself up to be restricted! You can extend the amount of time paint remains workable on a palette by covering it between painting sessions: I do this by setting Clingfilm (plastic wrap) over the reach and crushing it around each mass or puddle of paint to take out any air bubbles.

THE END